THE PAINTED CLOCK

MERCER UNIVERSITY PRESS

Endowed by

TOM WATSON BROWN

and

THE WATSON-BROWN FOUNDATION, INC.

THE PAINTED CLOCK

and other poems

Stephen Bluestone

MERCER UNIVERSITY PRESS | *Macon, Georgia* | 2018

MUP/ P564

Published by Mercer University Press
1501 Mercer University Drive
Macon, Georgia 31207

9 8 7 6 5 4 3 2 1

Books published by Mercer University Press are printed on acid-free paper
that meets the requirements of the American National Standard for
Information Sciences—Permanence of Paper for Printed Library Materials.

ISBN   978-0-88146-655-3
Cataloging-in-Publication Data is available from the Library of Congress

for Mary Jo

"... *so tangled up in you,*
so gathered in your arms,
I dance no steps I've ever danced
before this dance we do."

CONTENTS

ACKNOWLEDGMENTS

The following poems, many in earlier versions, have appeared in various journals: "After Channel Firing" and "The Ghosts of the Somme" (*The Sewanee Review*); "The General Slocum Disaster" (*The Atlanta Review* and *The Thomas Hardy Journal*); "Waltz" (section xvi of "The Painted Clock") (*The New Criterion*); "The Runner" (*The Hudson Review*); "The Scribe" and "Bogart's Face" (*The Atlanta Review*); "Healthcare Debate" (*The Satirist*); "Ichiro 2015" (*Aethlon: The Journal of Sports Literature*); "On the Sea" and "*Adon Olam*" (*Midstream*); "Mad to Be Saved" (*Measure*); "Jerusalem: A Vision" (*Mizmor L'David Poetica Anthology*); "The Lower Ninth" and "Federico García Lorca Visits the Sephardic Cemeteries of New York" (*From Neza York to New York: A Bilingual Anthology of Mexico City and New York City Poets*; reprinted in *Letra Franca*).

For their invaluable advice at various stages of work on this book, I wish to thank Alice Twombly and Zev Shanken. For guidance on matters technical my gratitude to Keith Bluestone is boundless. My greatest debt is to my wife Mary Jo Bluestone, who dances a new dance every time.

I. The Painted Clock

"The clock!" he said, suddenly slapping his brow. "Of course, that's it! A station without a clock is not a station."

In front of the other Germans, who were stupefied, he sent for the carpenters. He explained to them what he wanted: a clock face with hands, painted on a wooden cylinder twenty-eight inches in diameter and eight inches thick. Just as he was getting ready to dismiss them one of the carpenters asked,

"And what time will it be in Treblinka?"

Lalka did not understand immediately and the carpenter explained. "What time will the hands point to?"

Lalka hesitated and then suddenly looked at his watch. It was three o'clock in the afternoon.

"Three o'clock," he said.

Untersturmführer S.S. Kurt Franz had just stopped time in Treblinka.

— Jean-François Steiner, "Treblinka"

"There's neither woods nor trees in the wilderness."

— Treblinka survivor

THE PAINTED CLOCK

i.

It's us, isn't it?
And yet, when You make up Your mind to return,
to leave the shadows and to enter this room
with its plain fixtures, when You

emerge at last from Yourself, come down, look around,
loosen Your collar, meet the neighbors,
exchange pleasantries,
share the evening,

when You too ask us
to recount our journey to the station
with the painted clock,

O never mind that other place
with its endless Sabbath and adoring choirs,
O stay awhile, be with us once more.

ii.

Some say You're the first droning cicada,
old lettering, a sect. Some say
You're mad, the laughing-sliding of coal
down chutes into bins. Some say You're the palest blossom

of the earliest flower.
Some say You're wind, rain, and sky,
whatever swims, flies, or crawls,
hisses, sings, or speaks. Some say You're a name

that cannot be spoken. Some say
You're a sword and that if none remain in the hills
it's because of You.

Some say it was You at the siding
and when the valves opened.
Some say there was nothing else to breathe.

iii.

There were many villages on the way,
and the faithful, who stared
as we passed, seemed to know who we were.

No, it's certain, they knew us, for sure.

Along the route, crowds turned to watch.
How did they find out about us, those witnesses?
Who told them what was happening?
Had they been gathered, too?

"Is it You?" they asked, astonished,
as the cars rolled by, and they heard voices.

"Look, the river of God runs full!" they exclaimed,
as the trains went past their fields.

The land of the witnesses prospered,
and their wagons grew fat. After the harvest,
they danced and sang, and their markets flourished.

iv.

We faint with thirst.
The heat is unbearable.
There's no room to move.
I can't turn away.

There's no space between us.
You're here, too, I know it.
We're face to face.
We look each other in the eye.

We've never been this close before.

I've always wanted this, haven't You?

I also know You're not here.

I'm sure only of three things:
this heat, this thirst, and this journey
to where You are, which is where we're both going.

v.

Infinities, advocates, and seraphs, choirs of minions,
stand to the left and right, attendants
whose voices are tuned to a pitch as rapturous as the Name.

Theirs is the original tongue.
"Arise," they sing. "Comfort the sick."
"Deliver the oppressed, bring justice to the world."

And You hear them. You listen carefully.

(Such are the presences,
among whom, as they come and go,
we must also include the Angel of Death.)

In Your grief at the edge of the pit,
in Your quicklime vat, Your boxcar, Your tree,
their songs console You.

vi.

A wrong word is a wicked angel.

The words must be perfect.
"That's only beautiful," I think.
"That truth is partial," I say to Myself.

After so long, an eye blink, I still brood.
Full of misgivings, ill at ease, I have second thoughts.

After a little rest, no rest at all –
everything about it needs to be fixed.
I go over it again. I turn it over in My mind.

Every word matters: "freedom," "choice," "will,"
"seed," "grain," "leaf," "eyes," "mouth," "hair," "smile," "joy,"
"sky" . . .

"I spoke too soon."
"It takes greater skill, better judgment."

It requires deeper study, more time than I have.

vii.

When we were called, the angels
gathered in the air above the town square
watched, with their tiny valises, safe in their names.
How did they do it, the winged ones?

The language, as everyone knows, of heaven
(its everlasting bureaus, departments, jurisdictions, and courts,
its radiant agencies and authorities)
is, as sung by assemblies of guardians, stronger than ours.

The angels are called "Assured of God"
or "God's Favorite" or "God Will Heal Me."
The angels have names like "Ezekiel," but more powerful.

At the appointed time, when we're gathered,
"I Am Not Whom You Seek" is their name.

viii.

With a scribe's cupped inkhorn around his waist
(though some have said that his medium is tears),
an angel enters the world; he carries a whip,
and his commission is to circulate among the living
and to apprehend the specific owners of names
as set down in the strict process of his written charge.
"Once, you were favorites and delighted me,
but now it's time to come along," he says.
And so, leaving our villages, our homes, our lives,
putting everything aside, we rise like birds,
like a great lake of birds, and we follow him,
and soon, after a while, we arrive at a door.
"Enter here," the stern official says, with a smile.
"Now taste the bread of angels," he lies again.

ix.

Dogs bark.
The station's ready.
Everything's prepared.
We're right on schedule.

The cars roll in.
Whistles blow.
We spill out.
The siding fills up.

We've arrived.

Across from the entrance
is the face of a clock
whose hands point to "Three."

"Hear, O Hear,"
the painted clock says.
"You belong to me." "You're mine."

x.

As words that spoke to nothing made it live
with shouting, laughter, shadows, rocks, and leaves,
with lightning, lilies, waterfall, and snow,
so did the freighted cars in which we came,
filling the wilderness through which we rode
with echo, dream, time, star, and dawn,
dust, whisper, fog, smoke, and glass,
rainbow, stillness, singing, mist, and dew.
So loaded down, so jammed, when it arrived,
each car disgorged the cargo it contained,
of wallets, shoes, watches, hair, and teeth,
desert, drizzle, thunder, ice, and clouds,
unpacking bracelets, collars, coats, and wigs,
with woods and trees, and everything in heaps.

xi.

To pray is to go in all directions at once.
I pray to my refuge, tower, rock, and these,
in turn, pray to me. We pray to each other
for signs, omens, reflections in a glass,
as we pray for health, prosperity, and life.

We pray with all we are for thunder and lightning,
as we pray for frogs, blood, ease, and shattering,
for destruction, conquest, salvation, rescue, and sleep.

We pray to kill, to stay ourselves from that;
we pray for sweet death, for the end of days,
as we pray to survive, to outlast, as we pray for strength.

What in the skies compares with us, as I pray
to You and You pray to me, and we pray together
and to each other, in a wilderness under a clock?

xii.

Once I loved You and fought for You;
I carried Your banner everywhere.
Your cause was just; my scars made me happy.

And then I grew sick of it.
"Tell others about Your shield," I said.
"Find Yourself another killer."
"Whatever happens, I'll stay where I am."

But, look, Your enemies
prowl the streets, time has stopped,
and those who detest You prevail, howling like dogs.

So, yes, I see what's happening.
There's no one else – we'll both die.
I was a sword, quick on my feet and able to thrust.

xiii.

Time is a minister in the capitol of clocks
and sits at a desk, where, each day, he sets
the master clock, which sends its signal down the line.

When the signal arrives, it tells us what to do:
we work, we eat, we sleep, we stay to be counted;
we do exactly what the clock commands.

Tonight, in files, the stars line up and wait;
in dim official light, in standing rows, they wait.
A fine white ash collects, still incomplete, December, late.

Are You asleep? Are You as broken, too?
In the ovens of my cells, time bakes tonight like loaves,
like hard black loaves left in to burn.

xiv.

"Whom do you trust?"
"I'm Your servant, rescue me."
"Where do you live?"
"In You, preserve me."

"How can you not love Me as yourself?"
"This wilderness shames You."
"Do you think I lack compassion?"
"I live in the hour."

At dawn, high above me, I hear weeping:

"There are none but the two of us."

"I live in a ruin."

"All that lives is Mine."

(I've never been this attentive before.)

xv.

I know Your number,
and I know Your name; I notice everything.
I keep track of everything.

Are You watching me, as well?

When I say Your name,
I make a soundless sound;
I draw the letters in, then breathe them out.

(I'm nothing anyway.)

Watch out, they're all insane –
You'll need Your strength – no hiding place is safe.

Sooner or later we'll meet and never go hungry again.

(I sense this in Your face.)

xvi.

It must be *echt* Viennese,
with such and such an emphasis in the horns,
the second violins tuned lower
and the first higher, an old trick of ours.

It must be *lieblich,*
the time ever so slightly forced,
and have a brilliance (I know you won't understand this)
such that, in the *forte,*

it yearns.
You will play a caper in the air,
just as I direct you.

You will feign charm.
A certain delicacy is essential.
To falsify, that you know.

xvii.

I cannot tell
what whips and crops are at my feet,
what ash scrubs out the light.

Grounded, blind,
I wait in fright
among the razored thickets.

I peck and scratch,
I fret, I scrape, I hop,
I run the wilderness like any bird.

xviii.

"What is One, O Lord?"
Of actions and attributes, the words are endless.
If the way to You is One,
then this journey must be a single step.

Am I not near the end of it now?
Am I not almost home? If You are One,
then all going toward You must also be One.
When I arrive, will it matter how I have come?

As the dead in a heap, as strangling,
as honey and butter, so the distance between us
measures my progress through the world.

xix.

A child wept,
and someone said,
"Whip him, and you live."
So I whipped the child.

And I tried to pray, too,
something comforting, the words
I mean to say as I die:
"Lord of the world," I began.

Then another said,
"That one or else the rest, you decide."

After that:
"Two pardons for the three of you, make up your mind."

It's a lullaby and says the world will end.

I cannot close my eyes.

I tell you this whether you believe me or not.

xx.

Someone's shouting "Now!"

I must do as I'm told.

Will You go with me?
How will I know You from the rest?

When the door is shut, will Your voice
be more terrible than theirs, or the same?

When we're sealed in, will You cry out to Yourself?

Will I hear Your name at last?

I mean to be grateful. I dread not giving thanks.

These are my last questions.

To know Your name is all that matters.

(I can't tell, it doesn't matter now, as it disappears,
what color the sky is or at what feast
or in what other chamber the two of us will meet.)

xxi.

We're singing again – an old song.

The walls are thick, but surely You can hear us.

A song is a gift – it brings forth.
A song is the cornerstone of a house.
A people is a song or nothing.

Is that Your voice? Are You singing, too?

You're singing. You're singing. You're singing.

"There's no difference," You say,
"between your song and the dead."
"Your song is the howling of worms."

xxii.

The Sabbath-to-come,
the end of time, joy forever, eternal peace,
will I get to it from here?

I'm a simple man, no learning at all,
and what I know, I know.

The Queen of Days, the only Sabbath I know,
why change it for another?

If I had a choice, I'd keep the one I have.
I'm certain it's enough. I've nothing more to spare.

The Sabbath between the stars,
the day I love, I've stirred its light in wine.

The taste of it pleases me.

xxiii.

"My skin is an oven."
"I enter the pit."
"The snares of death entangle me."
"I'm poured out like water."

"You are my delight."
"Nothing's changed."
"We cannot live apart."

"I cower in ashes."
"My teeth grind on gravel."
"My eyes flow like a river."
"The vultures take me with ease."

"Our kisses are soul to soul."
"Our love is true, our hearts are firm."
"My words are never false."

xxiv.

It's quiet – the firing has stopped,
and the whistles, too. I can see the sky and moving clouds.

Beyond a crossing, there's a fence,
and, along a puddled road, a forest.

The rain has ended; there are no guards and dogs here;
I jump a ditch and enter a meadow.

I'm entangled with flowers,
and underfoot the earth is damp;
I struggle through the knots and blooms.

So far no one's spotted me,
and I enter the woods, where I burrow under leaves.

The underbrush will hide me.

The trees are all around me. I'm safe in the dark.

XXV.

It's a countryside full of streams,
with a palette of beech, larch, and pine,
where the birds make small talk
and the villages are full of children
who play among the gabled houses . . .

I love the everyday, its pretty music, its drone.

And yet – I hear it wherever I go –
there's a voice as sharp as the horn of an ox.

I hear it in alleys and streets,
through open windows, on the squares, in the shops;
I hear it in cafes, above the talk;
it reaches me in the lanes.

This place is hell, not hell.
Hell is a fortress with towers;
its dark gates and walls are massive.

xxvi.

Yes, I know I'm dust
and my days are a watercourse
and the stars burn out
and it all ends, sooner or later.

But the world is a lyre;
its music heals me;
its melodies comfort my soul.

A compassionate hand made it.

Even now, it thrills my heart.

Not a hood, not a blindfold, to speak of,
nothing but it, as it fills me,

as it takes me.

xxvii.

"You're safe, be sure of it."
"There's nothing to fear."
"I'm right beside you."
"Did you think I'd allow this?"

"Now breathe deeply, I require it."
"I'm steadfast always."
"Like a tall mountain, I surround you."
"To know Me is to live."

"Of course I'll do as You say."
"There's nothing else."
"I'm Your work, Your creation."
"I owe You everything."

xxviii.

Once the word for "clock" ticked.
The words for "clock" and "time" were the same.
We were just starting out.
We were learning Your language.

What was it You were saying?
Our portion, You said, would be "life."
"Eternity" would watch us from the sky.
The meaning of "time" would be "praise."

To learn Your language was everything;
without Your meanings, we knew nothing,
just clocks ticking, the sounds of machines.

The meaning of Your name is "unknowable."
Your name is Silence. Your name is Absence.
Your name is Something. Your name is Nothing, too.

xxix.

What dove in the piping,
jewel of an eye, sapphire in milk?
What crown? What arm?
Whose silver throat, singing, to me?

What lover approaching?
Whose torso, settling close?
Whose breasts, fragrant as spice?
Whose slender waist do I hold?

Is this our couch?
Are You entering me at last?
Are You trembling, too?

Whose lips on mine?
What taste in my mouth?
Whose sweet breath in my lungs?

Ashes of the Right Hand, Ashes of the Left,
our ashes, Yours and mine, fill the world;
we call our ashes *that which must be known.*

Ashes of Mercy, Ashes of Righteousness,
as grainy dust, as flakes, as settled plume,
we're everywhere at last, we veil the stars.

Ashes of ashes, of ashes, of ashes of ashes,
our whitened ashes blanket everything;
we contemplate their meaning day and night.

Ashes, ashes, ashes, ashes, ashes,
the more we seek to know, the less we learn;
we're blinded by the smoke of what has burned.

We signify, we name, we unfold what we know;
our ashes in the fire are what we know.
We know nothing; there's no end to what we know.

II. And Still the Slaughtered Rose

AFTER CHANNEL FIRING

At dawn, still wide awake, we lay
Remembering the voice of God,
More like the guns than we could say,
More angry, too, as if the Word

That split the waters with one breath,
And made with loving-kindness light
And every creature of the earth,
The shining day, the blessed night,

Regretted it. And so we wept,
Our empty sockets filled with tears,
Though no one heard, the living slept
The weary sleep of warriors.

Until a round – and then they woke
To a whistling out of deepest hell,
Grabbing for masks as the deadly smoke
Quickly scattered, clinging, from the shell.

One whiff of gas was all it took,
And the living clawed the air and cried,
"O Christ, come quickly, save your work,
Preserve us now, for whom You died."

"Have mercy on us, Lord, your own,"
They wailed. "We are the least of yours,
Who suffocate, go blind, and drown,
Gagging and burning, with blisters and sores."

All this in airless coffins we heard,
Though lidded tight for centuries:
The living judged before the dead,
But harrowed first, and then at peace.

And so we gave up wondering,
And settled down again to spend
Eternity unquestioning,
In a neutral darkness with no end . . .

And still the slaughtered rose in tides,
From Ablaincourt to Miraumont,
Where God for every one now chides,
In trenches on the Western front.

THE GHOSTS OF THE SOMME

on the eve of the Second Gulf War

at exactly 7:30 a.m.
on July 1 with a ripping fire
from bunkers and nests
the slaughter came down like a towering wave

the half hour struck
from Courcellette to Flers like a chime
in a cabinet engraved
with images of beetles skulls and crosses

at Ancre and Thiepval Ridge
on the salients of Gommecourt and Mametz Wood
men dropped like weights
or dancing first tumbled in all directions

the slain were everywhere
the trenched fields shook with mines
and in the flares at dusk
each soldier saw a double of himself . . .

and tonight too as we talk
flat on their bellies silent as worms
the anxious dead
still helmeted draw near us in the dark

under the pearly moon
with faces corked they hear us say
at the crack of dawn
the dead be sure of it will die again

THE GENERAL SLOCUM DISASTER

"Cover my defenseless head,"
the hymn on the program said,
"with the shadow of Thy wing," on the seventeenth excursion

north from Germantown,
of the St. Mark's Sunday School,
sailing up the river, from the tenements to Locust Grove,

an outing in the heat,
with a band aboard to play
"America" and *Unser Kaiser Friedrich,"* too.

Mixture of the old and new,
of "Under the Double Eagle"
and "Hip Hip Hurrah" and "On the Beautiful Rhine,"

such music, holiday tunes,
with waltzes, gallops, and marches,
was meant to entertain, a pleasant counterpart

to the *lieder* that were sung
as the ship undocked and turned,
on its way toward Hell Gate and then Long Island Sound.

"Let me to Thy bosom fly
While the billows near me roll,"
the children sang, to the Ground of Being, to the Rock of it.

To the Lord of Melody,
who, throned above the choir,
and, listening with interest, heeds but hides

(Master of the Universe,
    of darkness and of light,
whose brawny utterance alone made time and space),

    and who, afterwards, will save,
    though Pilot now of the spun
and lung-filled passion down, the spiral cruciform . . .

    As perfect as a rose,
    their mother-made flesh,
like thunder in a bell, sang to the Preserver,

    who took note, but said "This first!"
    and saw them as they sank,
tossed from the burning deck and bound to rotten floats.

    In that airless dismal murk,
    He watched His pretty work
in their slow fall, and, after the oil-spread fire, received them.

FEDERICO GARCÍA LORCA VISITS
THE SEPHARDIC CEMETERIES OF NEW YORK

The autumn stones spoke an Iberian patois
drawing the poet like water that weeps
to a distant port of myrtle and pomegranate,
though the dead from Recife in their linen vests
sang only of leaves, the small debris of leaves.

The sails of the boats were green and scarlet,
and in their holds a cargo of skulls slept
like autumn birds in an air of expectant footsteps;
the poet, listening, heard a song in the East,
saw a gate of gold and a hill bright with olives.

He saw frost on the way from Brazil, a pelican sea,
a pale moon off St. Pierre and Martinique,
and the fever quartering in, the rats of Spain,
the futile squadrons of doves in a dead cloak,
the artillery of waves, the furnaces of arabesques.

Many ships he saw downtown on West 11th;
on St. James Place, the hospital of the Alhambra;
on West 21st Street he saw St. Francis weep
in the chrome face of the stainless moon,
rising through latitudes, until it reached Granada.

To win himself. To conquer and reconquer
the sword of anguish in the shattered heart.
On the long road home from New York,
to refuse sleep until the bullet that made Christ,
magnified and sanctified, sang in his throat.

THE RUNNER

for Louis Simpson (1923-2012)

After the Caroline church and the colonists' common,
willow oaks and potato farms, you lay
beneath a cedar branch, and your gnarled hands
went east and west like sunrise across the boughs.

Safe at last. Or not. It's been six years.
And you, runner, frightened, quick, who survived
ambush, fire, slaughter, the worst there is,
where are you now, what governs your dreams?

The salt-rose clings. The dead of Hauppauge,
old neighbors, tumbled stones in your path,
they ask, too, who heard your steps in the grass,
in graveyards on the North Shore ledge.

And *camerados* in the lanes, the everyday ones.
"The runner," they'd say, "we saw him with his dog."
Lacking real news, they welcomed you,
and, soon enough, they got it, full on, straight –

accounts as clear as witness ever gave,
alarming bulletins and tidings of despair,
and every item just as dangerous
as if another Chekhov wrote it down . . .

But who, with wounds as terrible as yours
survives a peace? What frightened runner swerves
to a house that wheezes, I swear, like a fat man
in a chair, asthmatic as Port Jefferson?

"*Il dolce suono*," you might say, "the beauty it makes."
"Trapped in a fight, a dog-face has to breathe."
"These tracts and cindered spaces subdivide,
yet windows open, and lives reveal themselves."

And so let's say tonight you're at the desk,
at work as usual while the world's asleep,
and a page fills up, a scrawl goes to the edge,
while, across the room, an angry figure watches.

"Once, strange kind, my own cases kept me up,"
your father, in his lawyer's robes, remarks.
"And followed all the facts," you shoot right back,
spoiling as ever, despite how late it is . . .

Tonight an enemy commands the ground.
"You'd try to dodge me, runner, if you could."
Tonight the sentry of the guard cries, "No!"
You cannot go. The final word is "No!"

MAD TO LIVE

Leo Tolstoy at Astapovo

In the stable, no time to spare, he grabbed the harness.
Come dawn, it would be too late, and the light,
winding around him like smoke from a *muzhik*'s hut,
would trap him at home. *"To the farthest possible!"*
And his shivering friend answered, *"Bessarabia!"*
So they drove in the freezing dark to the Tula station,
escaping by train to Scheckino and Kozelsk,
then a carriage to the convent at Optina Pustyn,
until, growing feverish, he came at last to the edge,
to Astapovo, the last place, his final stop.
And the more he weakened, the more he hated to die,
since the everyday, he knew, was everything,
and everywhere, in cities, in little villages,
stupendous tales were gathering, begging to be told.

MAD TO TALK

after Doré after Cervantes

A nocturnal discourse. One of the Don's arms
around Sancho's shoulder, the other raised for emphasis,
the moon full, while Rocinante and Rucio,
indifferent to genius, rest in a clump of grasses.
The towns of Castilla-La Mancha sleep in silence;
the dispirited Dulcinea, ready to close her eyes,
calls it a night in wretched El Toboso.
Dulcinea has had it, but not the inspired Don,
unable to contain himself, who's just warming up
out here in the saffron fields, among the lakes
of Alcazar de San Juan, under the vigilance of the moon,
where he explains more clearly than ever before
exactly what *Truth* and *Beauty* and *Justice* are,
needing words, of course, but dreaming as he speaks.

MAD TO BE SAVED

Christopher Smart to Jack Kerouac

The road's rough, Jack, yet we keep on;
we burn and testify; we yawp non-stop;
we stay the course; we ride, no matter what,
two spirits in irons and lashed of the Lord;
our winding paths, I know, will reach the shore,
the restful end, the promised all-is-well.
Listen: *bell well toll soul lawn moon boon...*
You and I, my friend, are nightingales
who rhyme in syllables of tongues beyond,
in melodies, I swear, of time to come.
I stopped the other day with Mr. Pope
— a true poet, a blossom in God's eye —
and watched the flowers on a trellis turn.
Those Twickenham roses knew their gardener.

SKY TOMBS

for Seaborn Jones (1942-2014)

A *local surrealist*, hooded, grappling staves,
in the early morning you'd climb, hand-over-hand,
and mount, rung by rung, up past clouds;
sometimes with others, cloaked, you'd wait
at a sweet gum or an ash until you were called
or, from a limestone ledge or the branch of an oak,
in woods west of Lizella, go up alone;
once I saw you leave from an Indian Mound.
But always, after distant stars and moons,
old mysteries and secrets, you'd return,
come back to wars, catastrophe, suffering, pain . . .
This troubled world still needs your healing lines.
You left a strangeness behind when you left for good,
keeping the poems of it forever to yourself.

GOD'S GREAT HOSPICE

for Joyce Dykes (1944–1996), poet
(at St. Cecilia's Church, Boston)

It's weeping, from a jamb, in neon light,
that music-saint again, with mournful eyes;
it grieves her that the poetry has stopped;
she hates the squawk, she cherishes the lines.
"In God's great hospice, all this noise," she sobs,
an ear to end all ears, who loves the forms,
an innocent whose murder touched the heart,
whose silent singing drew an angel down.
You'd have to be stone deaf to miss it:
a good poet's gone, all the notes are wrong,
the words themselves mean less, the world is less . . .
Later, buses grind, a squall approaches,
and morning traffic out of Logan climbs.
A slow tin dripping calms her when it rains.

THE SCRIBE

for Donald Hall

And when the last imperfect draft is done
and the steeple of a Danbury church rings out
its knell, and death, preoccupied with wars,
puts you aside for now in his dusty stacks,
a vast *scriptorium* supplied with nibs and quills,
and then, like an old distracted farmer
neglecting his minor household chores,
forgets he ever left you with his books . . .
Who wouldn't want to spend the rest of infinity
restoring scrolls, re-inking faded alphabets,
rejoining broken ligatures and curls?
Who wouldn't want to wander among catastrophes,
mending the names of sex, love, and loss,
returning the vowels of compassion to utterance?

SECOND NIGHT SEDER
AT THE PUMP HOUSE

It's second night, and I'm at the Pump House,
a guest of Charles, who's invited me, and his friends,
and Charles, across from me, is telling a joke
everybody knows, but at which we all still laugh.
Around his head, I want to say, is light,
a halo scored like a cracked mirror on a fence,
while outside, along the tracks, it's all pine,
with dogwood below and azalea at the edge.
But then, just before the ham and greens arrive,
Charles stares back, a question in his eyes.
I'm here, I answer with mine, *and this is right.*
"Tonight you really took a turn," he says.
And then, to rest of the table, "So now let's eat!"
Which is how, second night, our festive meal begins.

THE CASTRATI

*"... and yet I owe for the flesh in the tongue
I brag with."
– Ahab*

"Long live the knife!" someone cried, as the aria rose

to another world:
Orpheus' pain, Hercules' madness
– the *appoggiaturas*, the trills, the coloratura –
the music fell from heaven. Cimarosa
and Gluck wrote for them, sublime music for monsters,
the treasures (some said) of the age and the gifts (others claimed)

of little boys to God.

You found them in chapels, in chambers, in halls,
and even the Emperor, who, on pain of death, abolished castration,
wept when his favorite sang. Yet choirmasters

kept auditioning prospects,
and the Duke of Mantua scoured Europe
in search of youths who could sing by heart, learn *contrapunto,*
and ornament in the Neapolitan style.

In time even the tight English gave gold;
Caffarelli prospered, and Farinelli, too,
and Giovanni Velluti, near the end, grew rich, as well.

Though it was, at the end, that love-struck Romeo,
the most passionate one of all, greeted the eyes of the dawn,

Alas, like a capon, a swollen pig, a fat buffoon.

Still, it lasted for centuries . . .

(As, for example, the great Gregorio Allegri,
using doubled choirs in a *Miserere* written for boys
mutilated in barbershops, so affecting Mozart in Rome
that the young traveler, hearing the piece just twice,
wrote down every note of it. Long dead at the time,
Maestro Allegri, who, it was said, had been crushed himself,
and who had also set Lamentations, still lifted souls.)

But as for mad Ahab,
who, while the puzzled carpenter measured his stump,
asserted that we owe

for the flesh in our tongues,

Ahab might also have said (later on),
that we owe for voices etched into zinc then pressed into wax.
We'd owe, in Ahab's ledger, for Thomas Edison's talking doll,
as we'd owe for the words themselves.

We'd owe, in Ahab's book, on account, for everything.

It's astounding, when you figure it, what the charges would come to.

THE SILENCE

for Robert Bluestone (1947–2012)

and behind the house was an arroyo
rising to juniper with swells of apache plume
and sage at the edges with oat grass and blue mist
where you had often seen angels
among the lilac and the jasmine bloom
infinite creatures whom you loved eagles necked in gold

and this was Santa Fe the red and gold
of Sangre de Cristo another Andalusia an arroyo
that flowered after rain and sang like aspen in bloom
along sharp crests a glorious plume
to which Fra Angelico himself might have added angels
young lutenists playing in sacred mist

under a sky so brilliant it glittered like the mist
that rises from fountains of gold
among galleries lined with madrigal-angels
and flute-playing gods of arroyos
spirits who call down spring melt with swirling plume
exalted choirs that make Jicarita and Pecos bloom

and yet you saw neither stalk nor bloom
no maize-bringer chanting in mist
seed-bearing dancer serpent with eagle-plume
you heard no voice crying wait Robert wait what gold
what air what melody in this arroyo
astonishing fiddle song ravishing gourd of angels

painted turtle-shell rattle of angels
will keep you here preserve you for the bloom
when it comes to arroyos

turning meadows to horn-in-a-mist
dressing slopes in blue and white and green and gold
crowning peaks with shining plume

you heard nothing in your tattered plume
too broken even for angels
who praised Glorieta's towering gold
and Atalaya's red-hued spiked bloom
and who gathered that morning to help in the mist
where you were one of them then nothing in that arroyo

angels singing made Sangre de Cristo bloom
sacred plumage rode above the mist
and afterwards spring was gold in the arroyo

THE COLLECTOR

It wasn't that his superb antique Marconi receiver,
a squat superheterodyne with walnut veneer,
its face all dials, its Cyclops eye as blue as the air
on whose waves music rode in from the coast,

actually vanished. Still, no one knew how it disappeared,
along with his collection of Jiggs and Maggie
and Mandrake the Magician, an illusionist who,
with Lothar and Narda, defeated evil; sky-writing

went, too, melting away like a witch in a bucket.
Yes, it was strange, his entire collection slipped off:
fish-tail bumpers, bubble-shaped fenders, toy soldiers,
metal pop guns, model trains and their stations,

all gone; even Tom Mix and Tony, Tom's wonder horse,
went, like a set of keys, as casually astray as the rest.
Gone, too, were the Wigwam Bar, with its red stools,
the Bondy Brothers Barbershop, and George Otis,

a mechanic who owned a garage and fixed bicycles.
Likewise Malone's Market, tulip-glasses at Woolworth's,
and the waitresses who worked behind the counter;
these all disappeared as if they were one thing . . .

And then it was autumn, with mums lining the walk
and the maples on both sides of it blazing like torches;
watching from his favorite chair in the windowed bay,
the collector suddenly remembered what he saw.

I've seen it before, he cried, as the morning light
slanted across the lawn, past the hedges, to the road.
Yellow poplar, red maples, white mums, he said,
wondering how he'd lost them in the first place.

That autumn morning, the collector gathered the light
and put it safely away; to everyone's surprise,
he seemed himself again, but then the light,
with all the rest, went quickly missing, too.

AUNT ESTHER

at the Jewish Home for the Aged,
on W. 106ᵗʰ St., Manhattan

It's late August, '72, and my aunt is reading
The Catcher in the Rye for the first time;
she's eighty-nine and fondly recalls the Lunts,
the carousel, and those ducks on the lake in the park.
Meanwhile, on West 106ᵗʰ Street,
street lights flicker and alarms go off;
it's nearly dusk, and, from where we sit,
you can also hear the sound of breaking glass.
"Holden Caulfield's doomed," my aunt exclaims,
on the run herself in a safe and tidy room,
almost at the edge, impossible to stop.
Aunt Esther walks me out as far as Columbus.
Tonight the sweltering city wants to burn.
A few at the corner stare, some nod, as we turn.

HEALTHCARE DEBATE

> *"Eliminate all government restrictions on the pro-*
> *duction and sale of pharmaceutical products and*
> *medical devices. This means no more Food and Drug*
> *Administration, which presently hinders innovation*
> *and increases costs. Costs and prices would fall, and a*
> *wider variety of better products would reach the*
> *market sooner. The market would force consumers to*
> *act in accordance with their own – rather than the*
> *government's – risk assessment. And competing drug*
> *and device manufacturers and sellers, to safeguard*
> *against product liability suits as much as to attract*
> *customers, would provide increasingly better product*
> *descriptions and guarantees."*
>   *– Hans-Hermann Hoppe*

Decrying the shameful want of good medicine,
Lionel Lockyer, licensed physician and chemist,
after long study and years of experiments,
offered, in 1670, a universal pill, a catholicon,
extracted in secret ways from the beams of the sun
and certain, in time, to root out all distempers.
Lockyer's patients brought fistfuls of copper
to his agents' shops, waiting in endless queues.
There were balms, salves, and elixirs, as well,
syrups of manna, cocoa, aloe, and urine,
distillations of calomel, rhubarb, and herbs;
there was no mixture too bitter or fantastic
for which the ill would not put out their coin.

Even Daumier's pharmacist, in *Le Charivari*,
made millions, or so he said, in only ten years,
from an ointment of suet and crushed brick.
Some of it worked of course, bringing cures:

opium antidotes, tonics, Kickapoo juice,
cordials, electric belts, and, most wonderful of all,
a celestial bed, in which, as its owner claimed,
a couple would conceive a beautiful child.
There were shows, too, uplifting spectacles,
and often an invocation of inspiring names
(*VesaliusDaVinciBrunoHarveyNewton*)
worked benefits as lasting as the medicine.

In wretchedness the body staggers on,
in constant fetters, as Lionel Lockyer knew,
as Texas Charley Bigelow and Colonel Edwards,
to their profit and amusement, understood;
Clark Stanley, too, a wrangler on the boards,
skinned rattlesnakes and boiled the yellow fat.
As sure as camphor, chloroform, and cloves,
a musked decoction, a mystic ambergris
– let the free and open marketplace provide –
it's easy money, the quickest score there is.
"No need to pay, although one has to live."
And the penny-pinching halt, with fists of cash,
came forward on their crutches to be cured . . .

Although from time to time the market slumps,
we die asleep, awake, at home, abroad,
we perish in a plague, a war, a dream,
we come at last to grief, despite all cures.
Misery's your winner when it comes to gain.
Add, I say, to suffering, go long on pain.

JERUSALEM: A VISION

after Blake, on a fantasy of Theodore
Herzl's about the conversion of the Jews

In Hammersmith the children lift their eyes;
in St. John's Wood and Paddington,
they shine, arise; in Amsterdam and Newport,
in Nottingham, these angels join in song.

Like flocks of brightest cherubs on the wing,
they offer sacred hymns; now Warsaw, too,
and Prague, one great metropolis of gold,
its alleys washed in blood that loves the world.

Too dark, too dark, the Synagogue of Satan!
"How can this be?" the stiff-necked ancients ask,
the bitter ones, the final generation,
who weep and pray outside St. Stephen's church.

Among enameled pillars high, the choirs sing,
in Hampstead and in Hackney, in Islington.
"Return!" the young ones plead. "Our nation thrives
in this exchange – our Zion grows in green!"

Take up the solemn Cross, O wanderers!
O rigid elders, O mournful patriarchs,
your jubilant and blessed babes proclaim,
"Come now – and not next year – to Jerusalem!"

ON THE SEA

after Jehudah Halevi (c. 1075-1141 C.E.)

Like giant seabirds' wings,
sails fill out in the gusts,
spreading, swelling, straining,
as the ocean boils like a pot

and waves spill over the deck,
rising to the top of the mast,
then crashing down from above,
like an army mad to kill.

This is the place of slaughter,
of the vicious jaws of night,
where the guiltless innocent
are crushed before they drown.

Whom shall I trust on the sea?
What pilot of the night?
What mariner? What friend?
What master of these waves?

What prayers can turn aside
the dark and indifferent world?
What desperate cries bring calm
to this wild and lunatic storm?

Like an ingrate, I've abandoned
the sweet blossoms of the sun,
the dearest joys of home,
to make this passage East.

I've lost myself and, worse,
the precious gift of love,
my daughter and her child,
the treasures of my life.

And for what? For the trace
of Jehudah to forget Jehudah?
Jehudah, the memory of Jehudah,
who rides the sea on a plank?

In time I may yet come,
a free man with uplifted face,
to stand before Your gates
and flourish in Your light.

May I flower soon, O Lord,
by the waters of the Jordan,
praising You who limit the sea
and grant the gift of mercy.

THE LOWER NINTH

Hurricane Katrina, August 29, 2005

"We rise," some sang, "in our infirmity,"
as it circled in from St. Bernard, surging higher
than in '24, when the levees were blown on purpose,
as spouts slammed through the steamboat houses
and it smashed Burgundy, Dauphine, Claiborne, and Royal.
It mounted into attics, corpses bobbed up and down
the Industrial Canal and wooden caskets
washed over banks and the living clung to roofs . . .
But worse than the turbulence of wind and tides,
sheltering justice, that rescues everything,
like a frail work that did not hold, then added:
"Now try to save yourself – you're on your own."
What shield, what help, what safety in the storm,
what defense against the flood or anything?

ICHIRO 2015

These days I'm sometimes good at what I was.
Still quick, mind you, I imitate myself,
an earlier version from a movie long ago,
with a sound track beating like a distant chime.
Four bats stand, handles up, near home plate,
and I, positioned just off second base,
in four successive attempts, knock each one down.
I was, in those days, a lightness on the edge,
climbing walls, snatching points on a moving line,
and everything I did was just a game.
Yet all it took to bring me down was time –
the more you live, the more it makes the rules.
The world's a playing field within the chalk,
and angels fly in pages of a book.

BOGART'S FACE

There wasn't much that make-up could hide
of the sag and droop of it, of the puffiness under the eyes,
and even in shadow no powder on thick base
could disguise for a minute the plain wreck of it
or conceal its actual age or what it said
about his real life or seem to revive
the corpse of its lids or with devious filter
soften to a pleasantry the truth it played . . .
Which is why you must forgive the last train out,
chaos at the station, the boom of distant fire,
ignore all properties of make-believe –
it's how you lift a shroud, strip off a mask,
at the moment you think you've done it right at last,
only to learn it's not true, nothing will change.

THE MUSES

for Gerald Stern

Accept, one said. Another said rise up.
Some were friends, as good, Montaigne might say,
as beautiful, though he, the best there was,
also never knew, in the end, what to make of them.
As for me, I cannot tell you what it was
or who they were or how they might have helped,
except to say that some were strict practitioners,
while others didn't care and hated rules.
I remember one who spent her life at home,
who loved the neighborhood and took her chances there,
that terra cotta look was something . . .
And build them temples, too, the ancients said,
who knew that some would later be in touch,
while some in your entire life you'd meet just once.

"THAT REEF AFFECTATION"

Now summer's gone, and light rides up
the wall again, throwing shadows on the sill;
I look up from the glare that spreads
across the page and glance across the yard
to its ragged fringe. I lift my eyes to drought,
to tree limbs down and pickets twisted
in the weeds, to vines that spread like wires
and choked the flats. For many months,
while the hedges turned to ashen brown,
I trimmed and shaped, trying for an effect,
avoiding what Castiglione, who defined
the art of seeming, called display or pose.
(And planted ornamentals, too, in pots
along the walk, and failed at that, as well.)
Death, when it happens, is meant to be;
it never merely performs; it's you, gardener,
as you want to be, immediate, yourself.
A child I love passed through, a dear friend
left a note, and I think I missed a call;
it's cooler now, but far too late to save
what perished then, what else, while I worked
to seem more like myself, I helped to die.

ADON OLAM
(Lord of the World)

after Solomon Ibn Gabirol (c. 1021–1058 C.E.)

Lord of the World, Eternal King,
almighty maker of heaven and earth,
the source and crown of everything,
yours is the sole dominion.

And when, at last, the world must stop,
your uncreated light shall shine,
eternal and invisible,
still radiant, still mysterious.

Lord of the World, you are the shield,
the only banner, of the heart,
whose limited comparisons
are all it knows to tell its love.

We watch in terror and in pain;
uplift our spirits, fill our cups;
we live in endings and beginnings;
our every thought is limited.

Lord of the World, Infinite One,
keep my sleeping soul from harm;
this life is troubling, cruel, and strange;
I rest in You, beyond all change.

NOTES

THE PAINTED CLOCK. The poem treats the journey to Treblinka (first third), the camp itself (second third), and the death chamber (the last third) and makes no attempt at factual witness or reportage. The detail of the painted clock, however, is true. The horrors of Treblinka have been documented by survivors, scholars, and in official reports. The poem explores the relationship between God and man within the framework, on one hand, of a supposed covenant between them and, on the other, the existence of a death camp. This is an inexhaustible subject that lends itself to many perspectives, including that of God, which may itself change from time to time, as the poem suggests. There is no single point of view, even at the end, among the survivors.

In its treatment of time in the death chamber the poem owes much to Ambrose Bierce's "An Occurrence at Owl Creek Bridge" and the 1962 film of the same name, released as *"La Rivière du Hibou"* (dir. Robert Enrico).

In section x the wilderness catalogue is somewhat indebted to the last stanza of an elegy by Georg Rodolf Weckherlin (1584-1653): "On the Untimely Death of Miss Anna Augusta, Marchioness of Baden" (*"Ueber den frühen tod Fräuleins Anna Augusta Marggräfin zu Baden"*).

THE GENERAL SLOCUM DISASTER. On June 15, 1904, the General Slocum, a steamship carrying 1,331 passengers on an excursion from Manhattan's Third Street Pier, caught fire in the cargo cabin near the bow. The passengers that day were members of St. Mark's Evangelical Lutheran Church, bound for the Locust Grove recreation grounds on Long Island Sound to hold their seventeenth annual picnic. Located on the Lower East Side, St. Mark's had been a major congregation since 1847 in the neighborhood known as Little Germany. A combination of a poorly trained crew, defective safety equipment, and general panic led to the loss of 1,021 passengers through burning, drowning, and trampling. This was the greatest single New York City catastrophe before the 9/11 terrorist attack nearly a century later.

This summary of the event is drawn from an essay by Zoe Simpson in NOT THE HUDSON: A COMPREHENSIVE STUDY OF THE EAST RIVER, created in the fall of 2011 by honor students of Fordham University at Lincoln Center under the guidance of Dr. Roger Panetta. Used with permission.

FEDERICO GARCÍA LORCA VISITS THE SEPHARDIC CEMETERIES OF NEW YORK. Lorca was in New York City from June 1929 to March 1930. Early in July he attended a service at Congregation Shearith Israel, originally founded in 1654 by Sephardic Jews fleeing Brazil. The poem *"Cementerio judío"* is dated January 18, 1930. As my poem anticipates, Lorca was murdered in Spain by the fascists several years later.

MAD TO LIVE. MAD TO TALK. MAD TO BE SAVED. See Jack Kerouac: " . . . the only people for me are the mad ones, the ones who are mad to live, mad to talk, mad to be saved, desirous of everything at the same time, the ones who never yawn or say a commonplace thing, but burn, burn, burn like fabulous yellow roman candles exploding like spiders across the stars . . . " ON THE ROAD, ch. 1.

SECOND NIGHT SEDER AT THE PUMP HOUSE. The origin of the second night Passover Seder has to do with ancient calendar issues for those living in the diaspora; for more than 2000 years, the second night celebration has been traditional outside of Israel.

THE CASTRATI. The epigraph is from MOBY DICK, chapter CVIII, "Ahab and the Carpenter."

JERUSALEM: A VISION. I shift the setting from Vienna (Herzl) to London and elsewhere and use the voice of Blake's address "To the Jews" in the prophetic book JERUSALEM: THE EMANATION OF THE GIANT ALBION. Herzl's early idea of mass conversion involved a procession on a Sunday at noon to St. Stephen's Church, where, "amidst the pealing of bells," the Jews of Vienna would convert to Catholicism. See THE COMPLETE DIARIES OF THEODORE HERZL, Vol. I.

"THAT REEF AFFECTATION". The title is an alternative translation of what Thomas Hoby calls "a sharp and dangerous rock" in Castiglione's discussion of *sprezzatura*. Castiglione defines the term as the avoidance of "affectation at all costs, as if it were a rough and dangerous reef, and (to use perhaps a novel word for it) to practice in all things a certain nonchalance (*sprezzatura*) which conceals all artistry and makes whatever one says or does seem uncontrived and effortless." THE BOOK OF THE COURTIER, I. 26. George Bull translation.

ADON OLAM. In Hebrew, as the sub-title notes, "Lord of the World." Sung at the closing of festival and Sabbath services since the 15th century C.E. I offer this version as a modern adaptation of a prayer that uses traditional and reassuring metaphors.